# UNLOCKING YOUR POTENTIAL

# UNLOCKING YOUR POTENTIAL

### IVY BLAIR

# CONTENTS

| | | |
|---|---|---|
| **1** | Introduction to Personal Development | 1 |
| **2** | Self-Awareness and Self-Reflection | 5 |
| **3** | Goal Setting and Action Planning | 9 |
| **4** | Time Management and Productivity | 13 |
| **5** | Communication Skills | 17 |
| **6** | Emotional Intelligence | 19 |
| **7** | Building Resilience and Overcoming Challenges | 21 |
| **8** | Developing a Growth Mindset | 23 |
| **9** | Building Positive Habits | 27 |
| **10** | Networking and Relationship Building | 31 |
| **11** | Financial Literacy and Wealth Building | 33 |
| **12** | Health and Wellness | 37 |
| **13** | Lifelong Learning and Continued Personal Developme 39 | |
| **14** | Conclusion and Reflection | 43 |

Copyright © 2024 by Ivy Blair
All rights reserved. No part of this book may be reproduced in any manner whatsoever without written permission except in the case of brief quotations embodied in critical articles and reviews.
First Printing, 2024

# CHAPTER 1

# Introduction to Personal Development

Imagine a world where money, success, and achievement are not at the forefront of everyone's thoughts. Imagine a world where mutual respect, love, and trust are the basic principles of interaction. The world would be a much better place. Personal development is the key to changing the way that people live. If personal development can help both the individuals and the world as a whole, why not get started on your journey towards personal development? Perhaps people do not choose to take the personal development route because they don't realize how beneficial it can be to them. Personal development is not about being the perfect person, but practicing ethical values and principles. It is available to everyone, and best of all, you do not need to possess a special range of skills to get started on improving yourself.

To get involved in personal development, you need to set your sights on improving the person that you are today. This is a challenging project and involves three main elements. It needs you to have foresight, imagination, and encouragement to change your life. Foresight is an important factor. You will never use personal development skills if you do not have a reason to use them. Once you have established the reason you wish to make changes in your life, you need to gain the relevant skills. In the end, it is important to remain true to yourself, without becoming selfish or ignoring others. People need to feel safe in your hands and believe that you are not going to misuse them. Success in personal development is not about seeking the encouragement of others. True success comes from knowing your worth and using it to create further success and achievement in your life. Once you get started with personal development, you will soon realize what a difference it will make to you and those around you. You'll be amazed at the results you find.

*Understanding the Importance of Personal Growth*

Everyone feels more fulfilled through growth. As with fitness, there are roles you can fill. It's not just enough to create economic value for yourself or help others directly; each of us is unique, and everyone has a responsibility to discover the skills and knowledge that express that uniqueness, that role. Fulfilling your duty will provide the satisfaction that comes with the innovation to create the greatest impairment-reducing benefit for the most people. People whose roles overlap and are in your Key Circle will help you on your path. The more demands present for your unique set, the more you can earn by filling those demands. These are the roles for which you are naturally shaped. Attitude is the root of success, with a positive attitude doing the most for cultivating personal success. One can achieve most productively through what is often called a winner's or growth attitude. It is absolutely important with a winner's attitude to know what your priorities are and always have this list in your consciousness, but do not become a slave to determined needs. Hence, balancing discipline with spontaneity and relaxation is essential.

Before we discuss our personal growth and the key variables that we can manage to improve it, let's discuss why it is important in the first place. What can personal development do for you? Whether you are an individual or a manager who cares about helping yourself or your subordinates realize great success, it is important to appreciate the potential major benefits of reaching one's full potential. It's critical to keep these powerful benefits in mind. The best time to plant a tree is twenty-five years ago; the second best time is today. Personal development helps build self-understanding and skills that increase Key Performance Indicators for people, with gains being greater than the investments. These KPIs include better health, happiness, growing success, longevity, productivity, and helpfulness to those around us. Personal development helps tap the overflowing fulfillment pool available in the universe.

# CHAPTER 2

# Self-Awareness and Self-Reflection

Self-awareness is the skill of being able to perceive your thoughts and emotions in the moment while understanding the long-term impact they will have. You can understand how you react and how others may view the reaction. This awareness is beneficial as it enables controlled behavior and language, avoiding regrets that may be said without thoughtful intent. It also enables an understanding of personal growth and where adjustments can be made to improve. Being self-aware allows interpreting the reason why successful events happen, and at times, the negative events too. By recognizing, accepting, and understanding, the reflections would not be necessary would diminish. No future project would continually waste time asking the same question because in your reflective familiarity, we have found the answers to guide the newly created clarity. Contains the power to build the top of Maslow's pyramid but the roots need the understanding of you.

Think about how you talk with your best friend. You don't have to think before answering, you just know what they want to hear because you are so in tune with that friend. You can become like that with yourself through reflection and understanding. You know what you want, you are not persuaded by others to compromise or do what they think you should. You have the emotional range to try new things. You accept that setbacks may be pushed back but you find resolution and a way to get things done. You are in control, understanding the responsibility of the outcome of your behavior.

With the principle that self-reflection and self-awareness are the key core to unlocking your potential, let us take a closer look. Being self-aware is about understanding yourself and your actions. You understand which behaviors and actions are in line with your values and are actively in control of your thoughts and actions. Doing this enables you to be confident to react without thinking, without hesitation. You have built the subconscious reaction because you have spent nights, months, and years repeating the behavior.

*Assessing Your Strengths and Weaknesses*

You can assess your strengths and weaknesses, using any of the following approaches. You can complete them all if it will help you to build a complete picture. Use an existing checklist. The questions you need to ask may already be available, in their most useful form. Checklists are included in many self-assessment books for managers. You can also use an evaluation form. This may be available through the organization where you work. This is the most powerful set of questions. You can also ask the ten most important people in your life. Then, look for consensus. Keep an open mind. Be prepared to learn something about yourself that you did not already know. Finally, considering your strengths can be hard work! Read over your answers to the questions on the last page. Then, ask yourself what you are best at and what rewards you with deep, lasting satisfaction? The answers to these questions will help you to discover your strengths. Then, relax and enjoy the rewards of your success. For the next six months, persistently develop your strengths, while avoiding significant distractions.

In this worksheet, you will learn how to assess your current strengths and weaknesses. This is the first step in personal development. Your strengths are the things that you already do well and enjoy doing. If you want to do them better, you can work at them for the rest of your life. You can build your life around your strengths. A weakness is simply something you have not mastered yet. It is easy to overcome a weakness. You only have to practice the necessary skills. This is the first part of the career planning process. Define what are your strengths and weaknesses, in these nine areas: Communication, Team Skills, Leadership, Management, Planning, Flexibility, Self-Reliance, Selling and Learning. You can also write about your achievements.

## CHAPTER 3

# Goal Setting and Action Planning

Goal Setting Setting goals is a way of organizing your mind and your time to enable you to make the very best of your life. Good, lively goals represent your real desires, and failing to use goals effectively can be a major obstacle to taking control of your life. If you set about your goal setting in the right way, it can be enormously beneficial. With goals set properly, and fulfilling their function fully, it's not just the process of working to achieve them that becomes more successful - your entire life can be transformed. Success is a matter of being able to recognize and utilize every single opportunity that passes before your eyes. Success begins in the mind, and when you grasp this concept, you realize that the limits you experience are based on your own preconceived ideas as to what is or is not possible. If you condition your mind to accept only the positive, your possibilities will know no bounds. However, personal improvement on any significant scale starts with worthwhile goals.

To be successful in any aspect requires action on our part. We can spend days, months, or even years of our lives contemplating what we want to achieve or the person we want to become, and that is as far as we progress. We never become the better person or reach the goals we set until we translate our thoughts into action. The secret to success lies in adjusting the focus of our thoughts so they are directed specifically towards what we desire to achieve. When we focus our thoughts in a positive manner, we provide ourselves with the tools of personal empowerment and action required to overcome the blocks we perceive as standing between us and our goals. One of the most effective ways to get this empowerment is to set yourself worthwhile, challenging goals.

*SMART Goals: Specific, Measurable, Achievable, Relevant, Time-Bound*

Time-Bound. It's important for you to set a timeframe for each one of your goals. Give the goal a target date and a sense of urgency. By setting a clear end date for each goal and breaking it down into smaller parts to be accomplished in specific timelines, you ensure that the goal will be accomplished. Not only can the setting of a time frame aid productivity within set timelines for a specific goal, deadlines also promote the further forward momentum of other goals.

Relevant. Making sure that your goals are relevant to your long-term aims is crucial. The origins of this goal are found over the course of other introspective processes. The objectives devised should follow logically from an overall purpose.

Achievable. A goal can be both high and realistic. You are the only one who can decide just how high the goal should be. So, it is important to set goals with the proper scope and difficulty. Challenging shall be provided, but making sure they are realistic and attainable will provide motivation and ensure that the process continues.

Measurable. Goals must be measurable. Be able to recognize when you are making progress and understand when you've completed your goal. Without some form of measurement, we have no way of tracking our progress towards our goal. Measuring progress is supposed to help you stay on track, reach your target dates, and experience the exhilaration of achievement that spurs you on to continued effort required to reach your goals. They also keep you in control.

Specific. Besides addressing important abstract values, you can also specify them using the question words what, why, who, where, and which. A goal without a plan is just a wish, so it is important to set down in writing and have a clear idea of what you are trying to accomplish.

The best goals to set are the ones that are SMART: specific, measurable, achievable, relevant, and time-bound. SMART goals are well-defined and easy to understand. Filtering your objectives through the SMART technique helps clarify your ideas, focus your efforts, and use your resources wisely. SMART criteria can also work in reverse. Using it can also help you recognize when a goal is too difficult and needs to be broken down into smaller steps. Setting a goal too high, for instance, can be demotivating, so it is important that your goals are realistic.

# CHAPTER 4

# Time Management and Productivity

Be comfortable in your own skin. Be flexible and manage demands around you. Only do things you love. Strive for work-life balance. Positive thinking is the single biggest contributing factor to creativity and problem-solving. Surrounding yourself with positive people will bring happiness. Set breakthrough goals. Attend symposiums and workshops to gain knowledge in your area of interest and technical proficiency. Always maintain integrity. Health comes first. If you don't have your health, you have nothing. Assess what is important in your life, then schedule your week accordingly. Find hobbies for enjoyment. Miscellaneous reminders.

Make a daily to-do list of must-dos. Visualize, believe, and enjoy the process. Trust and enjoy the journey to achieving your long-term goals. Be decisive. If you are stuck, the answer is simple: just make a decision. Set personal boundaries. Remember to learn to say no. Accept occasional letdowns and personality flaws, and you will be prepared to move on and progress. Commit to lifelong learning. Give up your time to volunteer. Positive thinking. Effective and efficient time management skills will make all the difference in how people work and how they feel while they are working.

With the time and technology available, we can all be very productive. Have you ever gotten to the end of the day, week, or month and felt like you haven't achieved your potential? Or are you burnt out every day, making sure everything is taken care of, and then having no energy left for yourself? Do you need to reprioritize your time? Right now, if you could pick one thing, what does success mean to you?

*Effective Strategies for Prioritizing Tasks*

Important but Not Urgent Tasks The important, but not urgent, tasks are the ones that most of us tend to skip, and we give priority to the urgent tasks that have a more immediate reward. Preventative measures or tasks, planning, and strategizing are often delayed until they later become urgent. The problem is that by the time they become urgent, they have evolved. The urgent becomes a crisis. The consequence is that the window of decision-making shrinks, panic reaction sets in, and everything becomes dire.

Urgent and Important Tasks The most important tasks have the most extraordinary impact on our long-term success. These tasks jump out at us the moment we hear them because they create consequences that can have a powerful and long-lasting effect. These effects are easily quantifiable and urgent. They make noise during the day and keep us awake at night. These tasks are often the most challenging. This creates fear, complexity, and mental resistance. They induce a fight-or-flight response.

Action Plan A good and well-organized action plan enables us to prioritize and complete our tasks within a reasonable time frame. We start with our ultimate goal, then create a series of tasks required to achieve the goal. These tasks are listed and ordered from the beginning to the final completion date.

The failure to have an organized plan of attack is one of the biggest reasons people fail in their tasks. Too often, people get caught up in the idea of doing everything they can to make things work that they do not stop and take a step back to see the big picture. What is most important? Do the simplest or most challenging tasks come first? It is absolutely essential to take the time to create an action plan and set priorities for your tasks.

# CHAPTER 5

# Communication Skills

Ways of ensuring that what we are saying is also being heard by the audience include speaking clearly, varying our speech, changing rhythm, and varying the tone of our voice. These are all indicators to the audience that this is a great story and is worth your attention. Your story can come alive with interesting variations in our speaking patterns. Pause before a pause. Tell the audience there is a reason why they should be really listening, so that the pause creates an air of anticipation. Often a good build-up of suspense saves telling the whole story and allows us to think on our feet and respond dynamically to our cues, thus making our story more interactive and our storytelling fun. It gives you the edge as well as making things interesting for everyone. Great storytelling is all about tension. We should deliberately build tension into our story. We become more powerful as storytellers when we heighten the tension by prolonging the resolution of a dramatic event. We then always keep this tension at our disposal to help us create the type of atmosphere we wish in order to get our stories noticed.

Earlier, we talked about nodding in order to show that you are listening to the speaker, with the added bonus for you of being able to keep your temper under control. Paying attention to a speaker is such an automatic habit that when we fail to do so, we should ask ourselves why this has occurred. It can be a useful warning sign that we have blocked the other person out because we are not liking what is being said. We hear the words but do not take in the message. In such a situation, a useful ploy is to use self-talk, wherein we are consciously saying to ourselves that we are not going to respond but will save those thoughts about them until later when we are alone.

*Active Listening and Empathy*

Empathy, the ability to understand and share the feelings of others, will differentiate you from the artificial intelligence with which you may be collaborating in the future. Collaborate and treat the person as you would like to be treated. Encourage collaboration, cooperation, and support. Ask yourself if you trust others and demonstrate the qualities you want to see in colleagues. Realize that in a knowledge economy, trust is a feature of collaboration, business success, and economic growth. Remember the very important correlation between trust and the ability to predict success. As for the quality and diversity of the relationships that you will develop in your personal and professional life, the index is built around respect, acceptance, understanding, teamwork, and confidence.

Recognize the importance of active listening and develop your skills by practicing the techniques listed below. Active listening consists of showing understanding, offering support, and taking an interest. A developer should be open to other ideas, look beyond their personal view, and be active and confident. Confidence and authenticity will take you a long way, and believing that you are an active contributor to society, that you have something worthwhile to share, and that expressing your own ideas and principles is good and important will also allow dynamic DNA. Authenticity is very powerful in the art of enhancing skills.

# CHAPTER 6

# Emotional Intelligence

Emotional intelligence helps to discern among emotions, which helps to keep our thinking lucid and our relationships honest, rather than projecting misuse of one's energy. It has been found that having a highly developed emotional intelligence can play an important role in our well-being and our involvement in a group's way of life. This is largely because people tend to come together to discuss reasons and talk over issues much more frequently than they get together to make monetary deals or ice a cake. Our impulsive life begins with the way we perceive each and every single particular happening around us. And like the ripple effect, if a few emotional uplifting gestures emanate from us, it multiplies and in turn does wonders for our well-being and the lives of our fellow human beings who live around us.

Emotional intelligence is the ability to recognize one's own emotions and those of others, to isolate the distinctions in our own emotions, and put them to good use, and to help others do this by stating one's dominant feelings and revealing one's distress with one's present situation. Society is riddled with a lack of emotional intelligence and it has resulted in many setbacks over the years. However, when emotional intelligence is strong in a leader, it can become contagious for all others in the chain of command, uniting everyone towards a common goal.

*Recognizing and Managing Emotions*

It is generally understood that emotions serve three primary purposes: Firstly, emotions help to determine the significance of situations and events. Second, emotions direct our attention and focus on the most important or relevant stimuli. And thirdly, emotions move us to take action and motivate us toward those actions that promise greater rewards. In this connection, they guide or inhibit our behavior.

But emotions are not only essential in understanding how we function. They are valuable tools as well. If we ignore, suppress or deny our feelings, we will not be able to release their energy. This, in turn, may lead to physical disorders and build up a range of negative physiological, psychological and social reactions. Recruiting the power in our emotions helps us to be more creative, make better decisions, improve the quality of our relationships at home and at work, and better manage pressure and stress.

Emotions are a natural part of our lives. They influence our behavior, from the way we interact with others to the decisions we make on a daily basis. Emotions impact not only our personal but also our professional development. The better we know and understand our emotions, the more confident we feel in managing the outcomes of our actions.

In this section, you will learn to recognize your emotions and the emotions of others. You will find strategies to help you handle negative and challenging situations, understand the role emotions play in conflict, and become aware of your emotional triggers.

# CHAPTER 7

# Building Resilience and Overcoming Challenges

Unlock your potential to build resilience and overcome any obstacle life throws at you, and you will, with time, be able to see opportunity in change situations that you would never have considered before. This capability to embrace and adapt to new and different pathways will open many new doors for you and help define your success, enabling progress throughout your personal, professional, and private lives. Ultimately, building resilience and developing personal coping strategies is part of any sustainable personal development initiative.

Resilience is the ability to bounce back, adapt, and transform your life in the face of new challenges. This increasingly important personal capability, which contributes significantly to success and well-being, can be cultivated. Resilient people become aware of emotions and can manage feelings effectively, develop coping strategies, and use their strengths to move on from challenging experiences, all thanks to the sort of coping competence that personal development develops.

*Coping Mechanisms and Stress Management*

Coping mechanisms relate to the way you react when faced with stress. Two key elements make up stress management: the first is preventing stresses from actually arising, while the second assists individuals in coping with stress when it proves unavoidable. In order to effectively manage stress, you need to understand the nature of the stresses involved. For many of us, effective stress management is the necessary first step towards achieving harmony and balance in our lives. A number of different models in different theories of personal development offer practical advice in this respect.

Here are a few tips on managing stress better:

1) Examine your thought processes by replacing catastrophic thoughts with less exaggerated and more realistic ones. Evaluate the most important life concerns that often detract you from your job and affect your other activities and behavior. After identifying the sources and kinds of stress in a better way, apply a systematic and problem-oriented approach to stress. This will significantly reduce the adverse effects of the stress.

2) Increase your concentration and the degree of personal control. One method of increasing the stress that needs to be acted upon without excessive worries is to reinforce the motivational state of your colleague.

3) If personal conflicts remain unresolved and the relationship with colleagues at work is less satisfying, the likelihood of your being stressed will increase. Trying to resolve the conflicts will help you maintain an increased performance level without unnecessary ethological stress.

There is no absolute right or wrong way of dealing with stress. The best methods to assist in mastering the art of stress control and management are practice and learning from your experiences.

# CHAPTER 8

# Developing a Growth Mindset

People with a growth mindset understand that achievement is largely about effort. As a result, they put in their best efforts and avoid looking lazy. Not everyone likes the idea of hard work, but they understand that improvement comes from practice. With a growth mindset, success comes from learning and putting in the effort, not from giving up, as in a fixed mindset. People with a growth mindset respond to failure differently. They don't take it as an indication that they are no good at something; they change their strategy, they ask for help, and they keep on going. They don't fear to fail and so are more inclined to take risks. They understand that failure can be a wake-up call and an opportunity for change, growth, and learning. With a growth mindset comes a desire to improve. With a growth mindset, you have good results because you are constantly challenging yourself and your abilities.

What is far more successful, however, is what is referred to as a growth mindset. A growth mindset is when we believe that we are continually developing and that the more we engage with something, the more we practice it, and the more that we learn about it, the better we will become. We set our minds that we are always working towards our potential, that we all have the ability to achieve far more than we are demonstrating at the moment.

We all have our own mindset about ourselves and who we are and what we can achieve. Many of the personal limitations we feel are self-imposed; they are only real because we believe them to be real. These are what are referred to as a fixed mindset. People with a fixed mindset believe that they are born with a certain amount of intelligence or skill and that this never changes throughout their lives. If they are not very good at a particular thing, then they feel that they will never be good at it, as if they believe that they have reached their potential and that's that.

*Embracing Learning Opportunities*

You can discuss value-added conversations with all team members. By exchanging knowledge and always learning, we are achieving important goals key to achieving successful leadership. Making the time to learn new trade skills, discussing family issues, relieving everyday stress, discussing personal experiences, etc. provide internally developed techno-savvy employees that are adept in the following skills: academics, social, and political knowledge; problem-solving challenges; group interactive focus on specific market capabilities. To return to an era of commonsense business change where talented leadership draws value-based knowledge from real-time experience, rewards intuitive relevant knowledge, and works from intelligence, drawing from past business experience.

Personal development is essential to your success and growth as a person. Developing your own personal development skills boosts your self-awareness and becomes a key tool for inspiring, influencing, motivating, and leading others. Possessing or lacking these qualities can prove a compounding base for team unity and ambition. What does informal learning through everyday mundane activities such as watching the news, reading the newspaper, discussing promising events, actively listening to others, or discussing business and market trends with peers do for you? It all leads to an increased awareness of world trends. These increased levels of awareness make you well-educated in the field of human capital.

# CHAPTER 9

# Building Positive Habits

Relate to yourself. The only person you will be spending every life with is yourself. You may be a hero and do not realize it! You will let people down occasionally. You will alienate some and amaze others. There are moments that will haunt you and moments that make you proud. You keep growing and develop a better relationship with yourself. The overall attitudes we are perceived to hold relate to how we value ourselves. One way to relate better to yourself is to grow and learn about things of interest to you. Pursue your hobbies or practice a sport. Keep your dramatic flair alive. Keep learning to keep growing personally.

Develop a positive outlook. Feed your mind with the positive. Read inspiring books. Watch inspiring movies. Spend time with can-do people, and be a can-do person. Five people think of you, stand within close gain to, and take an interest from, the average of you #-people. Develop a set of lifelong friends who form a positive community. They will support your ideas and your dreams.

The most effective way to turn a dream or a goal into reality is to develop it into a daily habit. To achieve success, it is essential to identify self-defeating habits and replace them with habits that will help you achieve your true potential. Here are some ideas that will help you replace negative habits with positive ones.

*Creating a Routine for Success*

As we've seen in some of our other sections, human beings function best when they have routines. We already have some routines in our lives - the things that we do when we wake up in the morning, eat breakfast, and head off to work. What we need to do is refine those routines so that they support and strengthen us. The key is to figure out how we are on our best days, and create a routine that helps us be our best selves every day. Here are some daily routines that help some people do their best work consistently:

1. Big block in the morning to do your most important work.

The brain is generally in its best shape in the morning, which is why most people should have a good block of work in the morning that lets them get traction on their most important project. This block could be anywhere from 2 - 3 hours. Likewise, even if you are a person who works better at night and starts work at 10 pm, have that block where you do your most important work at your most productive time and guard it with your life.

2. Exercise in the AM.

Little explanation needed. Consistent exercise of any kind of physical activity is essential to rejuvenate us, keep us in shape, and give us the energy that we need to do our best work. However, it's best to complete a session of physical exercise while our hormone levels are at their highest. If we exercise late at night, both our energy and sleep can suffer.

3. Two hours of strategic thinking.

This is more in line with the entrepreneurial spirit and does not apply to everyone perhaps, but for some entrepreneurs, thinking through big ideas or writing on industry trends is a great way to keep competitive. One could also do with two hours of reading to keep our strategic mind sharp.

4. Break for lunch.

You deserve it.

5. Responsiveness to emails or calls.

Choose a couple of dead segments throughout the day where you respond to emails or calls, say, 10 am in the morning and 4 pm in the afternoon. Email Bandwidth is a great productivity tool that takes only 5 minutes to install and will keep you in check. If you are managing a team or running a business, it's important to keep tabs and help remove barriers for our team. The rest of us would be better served just closing our email inboxes and checking it at pre-set times. Your company is not poised to crumble in two hours.

6. Learn and try new things in the afternoon.

Using the understanding of the morning energy levels and work that those high energy projects in the morning, keep less demanding work for the afternoon and spend the rest of the day improving and learning something new. A slightly more technical term is margin time where you use the time not used during deep work for things like arranging meetings or developing oneself away from work.

7. Treat evenings as evenings.

Again, assuming that one has finished the important work in the morning, treat evenings as actual evenings where you eat, relax, and sleep. The temptation to stay up late at night just because you do not have to be up in a couple of hours for work or school will take away the free time for your personal development and also affect your sleep habits.

A simple sentence such as, "After my morning exercise routine, I sat down and spent 2 hours working on that customer project that they needed so it does not eat up our leisure time later," becomes possible with this kind of structure. Remember that it's when you don't operate on routines where our energy gets sucked up on low-value tasks and under-the-radar distractions occur - which can take as much as 2.3 hours a day. Establish a routine at work. If this is something that you really struggle with, maybe performance stays poor, consider improving the way you organize your activities. You might be managing your work in a way that doesn't really match the way you naturally work. For example, we could work in a way where we need to step back, consider, and understand the theme of the project instead of constantly working.

## CHAPTER 10

# Networking and Relationship Building

How to speed up business networking. You can speed up your ability to develop effective strategic alliances. The real reason your small business or corporate sales effort is dead or dying is that you have no personal relationship with your prospects. It is an area where you are letting the marketing people waste valuable time and money with long shot programs and sales departments use outdated pressure tactics. Until you speed up the creation of your prospects' perception that you are a problem solver and have set up a personal following for both your project management delivery and methodology skills, prospects, business allies and competitors will continue to see you and your product or service offer as commodities to be compared and your prices will continue to be continually pushed lower.

Serious networkers generate hundreds and often thousands of business cards every year and find that introductions bring in lots of extra business. One golfer I know now has an annual event where players are required to stop play and concentrate on serious networking techniques at each of the golf tournament's 18 holes. After each game, he always has a new and lucrative business to add to his accounts list.

*The Power of Building a Supportive Network*

Everything you desire in life and in business involves other people. It is through cooperation that you progress and succeed. Without anyone to sell to, and consequently without anyone to earn money from, your business simply would not exist. It's therefore counterproductive to pursue a life of raucous independence. You can't do everything, so certainly don't try. Don't be the shy, reserved individual that sees others as competition for success. Instead, look to be the energetic, charismatic person who believes in the magic of interaction and finds the opportunity to further your success through others. Through coaching, encouragement, and support, you can develop a network of positive, successful, and motivated individuals who can push both you and themselves to achieve much more than you could without each other.

The people you surround yourself with can have a profound effect on your life. Their presence can influence every aspect of who you are and who you will become. The late Jim Rohn, America's forefather of the personal-development movement, summed up life's journey with this profound message: "You are the average of the five people you spend the most time with." That's why it's so important to pick those five people carefully. Determine them by understanding where your focus should be. Look around you, and examine your friends, relatives, colleagues, and associates. They reflect who you are, and furthermore, they hope to shape you or absorb the shape that you are offering.

# CHAPTER 11

# Financial Literacy and Wealth Building

Financial Literacy

Many people have no training in money management. School systems do not present financial literacy as a priority, and many people learn about money and money's management from their parents or close relatives. Unfortunately, many of those offering advice about money lack the background in investing to give such advice and thus fail themselves and those who depend on them.

Too many individuals live their lives in debt. Some lose their homes to foreclosure because they do not understand the simple mathematics showing that when their loan's interest rate (including points and fees) exceeds the appreciation rate of the home, they will soon lose both the residence and their savings already paid to the bank. The mortgage broker does not reveal that the loan has an adjustable interest rate that, within a year, will significantly increase the amount of interest due. These homeowners never knew to ask the question.

The same moves have cost life savings invested in the stock market or in small business operations. Many financial books and tapes exist, but few are written for the individual earning a typical wage.

The language used by the financial advisors is far too formal with far too many unfamiliar terms. Individuals describe their process for selecting an investment as something akin to playing the dollar bill slot machine. They contribute no more thought to the process than that required when purchasing a lottery ticket. Most important to note is that unlike the outcomes of totally random events, financial decisions may work out well; the investment may increase significantly in value. Learning about investing is not beyond the capacity of almost anyone. With a modest amount of effort, a young person beginning in a minimum wage job can become sufficiently knowledgeable to make smart money decisions.

Financial independence results when the money derived from your investment is sufficient to meet your financial needs. Wealth is the result of a sizable buffer that, combined with a lifestyle to match, can provide comfort on an annual basis for each individual plus the individual's family. If after following the directions laid out here, all goes well. Some investors become much wealthier than they ever dreamed. Their successes may inspire you to move beyond the first financial level outlined here and to emulate their strategies. Some strategies of the better, financially successful investors will be addressed throughout this book.

*Budgeting and Investment Basics*

Basic common sense: spend less than your income and save 10 percent of everything you get. This is an old adage that is proportioned to other times and places. If you want to save more, spend less. Free yourself from consumerism. The value of spending on personal and family happiness is not proportionate to luxury spending. This year's must-have item may become next year's junk. The value of the U.K. retail market is mainly based upon competitive spending driven by consumerism. If saving 10 percent of everything you receive is not attainable, assess whether you are living within your means. Invest as many times as your money can work for you. Squeeze out every drop of return in your risk budget. The 'investment' is our wealth creation. Make your money work for you and yield more. Utilize all tax shelters to get an additional return. Engage in tax and investment planning at the same time as creating your wealth objective.

Let's start with money basics - budgeting and investment. There are three reasons why budgeting is important: if you don't know where your money is going, especially nowadays when many of us use electronic banking and rarely see what proportion of our disposable income goes in cash payments, you may be overspending. Without a pre-tax budget, you won't know how much net income you will have for spending money after taxes. It is important to have an emergency fund to cover unemployment or other sudden financial needs. This should cover six months net income and all the non-discretionary expenses, and be held in a savings account. Although expenditure is subject to psychological influences on a person's perceived wealth, a savings-driven person spends what is left after saving.

# CHAPTER 12

# Health and Wellness

Your productivity and success in life are greatly affected by your personal energy and how you feel. An athlete cannot be productive in a professional capacity with a pulled muscle, yet a lot of business professionals work long hours and push themselves beyond normal capacity with minimal breaks and time for recharging. Everyone will at some time face challenges, and how you face those challenges with a sound mind and body is strongly affected by your fitness and well-being. People high in wellness take the time to manage their personal growth. They are typically confident, secure people, easy to talk to, and full of energy. They enjoy challenges and are self-assured. Research has found that low self-esteem, worry, and uncertainty affect job performance. They create a lack of motivation and can ultimately weaken every part of a person. Release stress; unfortunately, unlike a machine, we cannot always keep running and performing. The human body and brain need time to relax, wind down, and regenerate. Activities such as sports, meditation, and relaxation exercises are effective releases. Disengage. This involves taking a mental break, read something other than a financial report or a manual. Educate yourself in ways that may improve your capability in your profession or broaden your personal interests. Learn to unlock your potential with a life coach.

*Physical and Mental Well-being*

My concern is getting physical well-being. And I'm assuming that when you chose this book, you indicated your concern for personal development. Therefore, you have to admit, then, that my concern is valid in relation to you. Well-being. Let's not split hairs: if you're not feeling well physically, you are not well. And it doesn't become a living body, even though the doctors and scientists wouldn't agree that it's a living body! You'd die without vital organs, but these alone are not enough. A fetus immediately dies at conception. Engage any of these vital systems and, zoot, there you are a living body. Simple!

How physically active are you right now? Can you climb stairs without gasping for air? Can you fit into clothes that you like? Or fit into clothes at all? Do you worry that you will exhaust your partner if you have sex? Are you tired a lot of the time? Do you get frequent headaches and/or back or neck pain? If any of the preceding have made you uncomfortable – or feel smug about how fit you are – let me ask you whether you're also feeling that you're not getting as much out of life as you think you should?

## CHAPTER 13

# Lifelong Learning and Continued Personal Developme

Personal development is like any other human behavior, skills, or discipline; it is capable of improvement. Just about any behavior in education, life or work that if properly researched, is capable of improvement. Endless studies suggest that it is possible to develop aptitude, attitude, skill, and performance. Equality of life or work can be improved. This suggests that people can modify their attitudes, use aptitude achievement determinants, through personal development to effect a change or better skill, accomplishment, and performance. What about personal or self-development? Surely, this too can be improved? Developing an individual's capacity through realization, self-discipline, self-management, learning, training, and regulation could help develop this chosen direction and increase the natural capacity of the individual.

The world is a constantly changing place. Clearly, there are many reasons that society, the environment, and the workplace change and develop. Not everyone is always pleased about these changes. For example, new technology in the workplace has, in many instances, made existing jobs and skills redundant, and these changes have caused substantial resistance. The broader implications of this are quite clear. Corporations and organizations will use those who are willing and competent to do the work they believe is both necessary and essential. This often means staff that embraces new developments, adapts to and welcomes change, and has the skills most important to the future. This appears to be a set of circumstances that reduces staff resistance and business inefficiencies, and improves corporate performance and employee job satisfaction. It should be no surprise, then, that lifelong learning is an essential part of the personal development requirement. The outcome of the process is that through lifelong learning, it becomes possible to remain as a critical resource in the workplace, and hence become regarded as vital to the organization.

*Exploring New Interests and Skills*

Why not engage in a regular reading program, attend a course, volunteer your services, learn to play a musical instrument, take up a new sport, or order a 'how to' book and dedicate a part of your leisure time to do service for others in a manner of which you can be proud? Dare to try something which is new and different and draws you even though it might involve a small risk that you would not be good at it or that others would ridicule you for doing it. Most of the chores in life are to be tackled with an attitude of 'I can and I will'; but the interest that relieves needs accult definitely deserves a place in your overall life plan.

New interests can also provide balance to your life, as well as personal enjoyment. Many people devote all of their interest and time to either work or family and then wonder why they are always feeling frustrated or empty. Having a hobby or exploring different interests may also enable you to meet new people who might become friends or provide you with opportunities for fun and recreation during your leisure time.

Physical fitness contributes to success; without it, one's energy and alertness become deficient. Clean air, exercise, and inspiration from nature contribute to our well-being.

Discovering and developing new interests and skills is vital to your personal development, so that you can continue to grow as a person and meet the constantly changing requirements of work and family life. Continuous skill enhancement is essential to enable you to stay on top of your work. Anxiousness, discontent, and loss of self-esteem that can result from obsolescence or stagnation are unwelcome and unnecessary dangers.

# CHAPTER 14

# Conclusion and Reflection

If there is any sense in which we would like the authors to guide or mentor you, it would be in enabling you to access your own unique potential and wisdom. So how about continuing to work on bringing out these indispensable and valuable qualities in you? This book has been about the power of your own insights to drive real behavioral change that leads to success for you. Once again, if some of it leads you to acting differently and to seeing more of the kind of success you seek, and then peace and fulfillment would surely follow suit. The final word is this: "Success in many endeavors, he concluded, depended not just on the mastery of time, but on the mastery of oneself." Success then does not litter the path to achievement. It does indeed travel on the shoulders of personal development, but it can take you all the way, and when you get there, it's great!

During the course of this book, you will have been introduced to some powerful models for understanding and dealing with the world. However, arm yourself with just one of these and you can change your life. The answers you seek in life are within you and have been for centuries.

In conclusion, we hope that this book will have helped you understand the value of personal development in increasing your chances of success, not only in business, but in your personal life too. We have covered a diverse range of subjects on this journey, from developing the skills to communicate, effect change or lead others, to identifying what it is that you really want and pursuing your goals with the passion, commitment and focus that underpin all great achievements. Indeed, it is a lifelong learning and doing and being journey. We would like to conclude with some final thoughts on the book's themes before leaving you to dream big and live fully.

*Summarizing Key Takeaways*

For any individual to improve and grow as a result of training and development activities, a prerequisite is the identification of one's own strengths and weaknesses that are needed in order to highlight personal growth. Individuals must take responsibility for their own personal development and can use tools to assess and evaluate their own abilities to identify a gap between their current lead practices and desired historical practices. Goals should then be set to help achieve the desired new ideal state. Without the proper motivation to grow, an individual will not be successful at personal development, highlighting the importance of setting achievable learning goals. With this individual motivation, training and education can capitalize on existing motivation, abilities, and talents inherent within individuals.

There are several important takeaways presented in the personal development portion of this book. First, growth through learning from new experiences is achieved by building upon what you already know to generate new knowledge. Second, individuals can create change through the development of new mental models. The most effective learning occurs when individuals are empowered to actively participate in the process. Third, in order to help children and adults build upon their knowledge, both formal and informal education and training opportunities must be provided. Fourth, current and potential future teachers and trainers need to be open to the idea of teaching and training for growth in order to maximize and recognize their role as facilitators of this process.

www.ingramcontent.com/pod-product-compliance
Lightning Source LLC
LaVergne TN
LVHW092100060526
838201LV00047B/1492